A COUPLE'S LO

100 Things
I about US

Ketsia Gustave

ROCKRIDGE PRESS

First Rockridge Press trade paperback edition 2022

For general information on our other products and services, please contact our Customer Care Department within the United States at (866) 744-2665, or outside the United States at (510) 253-0500.

Paperback ISBN: 978-1-68539-925-2

Manufactured in the United States of America

Series Designer: Liz Cosgrove
Interior Designer: Tess Evans
Cover Designer: Tricia Jang
Art Producer: Melissa Malinowksy
Editor: Rachelle Cihonski
Production Editor: Jaime Chan
Production Manager: David Zapanta

All images used under license from Shutterstock

10 9 8 7 6 5 4 3 2 1 0

For: ....

From: ....

with lots of love

Date: ....

Author's Note

Welcome to *A Couple's Love Journal*! I'm Ketsia Gustave, relationship coach and blogger at EvolvingWife.com. Since 2015, I've dedicated myself to helping people build emotionally healthy relationships using practical advice and evidence-based research. Every day I wake up inspired by and excited about helping people open their hearts to giving and receiving love. This passion was born from my own experience meeting and falling in love with my husband.

Journaling about your experiences helps you stay grounded during life's more challenging times. This journal is a place where you can relive the most meaningful moments in your relationship and express gratitude for all the things that make your connection with your partner so special.

This journal contains one hundred prompts for you to fill out: seventy-five fill-in-the-blank prompts, ten "Top Threes," and fifteen "Moments." There are also Extra Love pages that you can use to include photos and mementos or to make notes and drawings.

This journal is meant to be filled out over time, so don't worry about trying to finish it all in a day or two. Take your time filling it

out in whatever order you wish, as you feel most comfortable, and gift it to your partner at any time. My hope is that this journal will serve as a collection of the moments that solidified the foundation of your love and friendship. This way, when the challenging times arise, you can come back to this book and remember that there is still so much to be grateful for and so much worth fighting for.

In these times, love is the one thing that gives our lives meaning and hope. The more of these moments you collect, the stronger you can stand in the midst of life's battles and uncertainties.

Love is true wealth.

Ketsia Gustave

1.

I LOVE LOOKING BACK ON OUR

FIRST DATE WHEN WE

....

2.

I feel confident our love is strong because

....

3.

One of the challenges I'm proud of us

for facing together is

. . . .

4.

I love that we try new experiences

together, like the time we

....

5.

Our favorite store to shop at is

....

because we are crazy about their

....

There's always room in the budget for

.... !

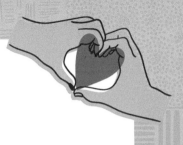

6.

I cherish our everyday moments.

For example, one of my favorite things

about our evening routine is

....

7.

When it comes to money, we make a terrific

team because we make sure to prioritize

....

8.

I love when we practice self-care

together by doing activities like

....

9.

I love it when we

....

with our family and friends.

10.

It's so much fun when we watch movies like

. . . .

11.

I love that we can laugh at one another's

weird habits, like

....

12.

I love that even the mundane stuff is fun

with us, like the time we

....

13.

ONE OF MY FAVORITE MEMORIES IS

THE TIME WE TOOK OUR FIRST TRIP

TOGETHER TO

....

"extra love"

14.

I love that when it comes to our careers, we both

....

15.

It fills me with joy when we celebrate one

another's wins, like the time we

....

16.

When our favorite sports team

plays or our favorite TV show comes on,

I love how we always

....

17.

We're on the same page in the things that

matter most. I love that we are passionate about

....

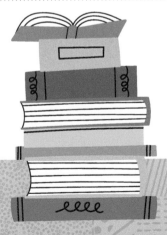

18.

I WILL ALWAYS REMEMBER OUR FIRST

ANNIVERSARY BECAUSE

....

19.

Our top three favorite restaurants are

1. ....

2. ....

3. ....

20.

I love how we inspire each other to

....

21.

Nothing makes me happier than when

we have a blast geeking out about

....

22.

Our nicknames for each other range from funny

to heartwarming. I really love when you call me

··· .

It's fun to playfully call you

··· .

23.

Our top three dream vacation destinations are

1. ....

2. ....

3. ....

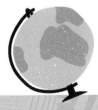

24.

I love that we can read each other's

minds when it comes to

....

25.

I love that we try new hobbies together, like

....

26.

We have so much fun doing chores

together, like

....

27.

Our top three favorite movie quotes are

1. . . . .

2. . . . .

3. . . . .

28.

Our favorite drink(s) to enjoy together

after a long day is

....

29.

I LOVE THAT ON OUR FIRST

VALENTINE'S DAY, WE

....

30.

I love how powerful our connection is,

especially during our first few months

when we would

....

31.

I love that we're on the same page.

Whenever we discuss our plans

for the future, they always include

....

32.

I love how we encourage each other to get

out of our comfort zones, like the time we

....

"extra love"

33.

Our top three goals we want to achieve are

1. ....

2. ....

3. ....

34.

I KNEW WE HAD INCREDIBLE CHEMISTRY

THE MOMENT WE

.

35.

When it comes to social media,

I love that we both

....

36.

I love that we don't take each other for granted.

We show each other appreciation by

....

37.

I love that we make one another feel safe

when it comes to

....

38.

I CAN NEVER FORGET THE MOMENT

WE SAID "I LOVE YOU" FOR THE

FIRST TIME BECAUSE

....

39.

Our favorite time of year is

....

because

....

40.

I love that we're intentional about

planning romantic dates, like the time we

....

41.

I love it when we go outdoors to

....

42.

Our top three favorite love songs are

1. ....

2. ....

3. ....

43.

I love that we can effortlessly open

up to each other about

....

44.

It's always so fun when we swap

childhood stories about

....

45.

I love it when we dress up to go to

....

46.

I REMEMBER SPENDING OUR FIRST

HOLIDAY TOGETHER WHEN WE

....

47.

I am so glad we both love to read and discuss

. . . .

48.

When it comes to intimacy,

I love how we always

49.

When we celebrate our birthdays,

we make each other feel special by

....

50.

THE FIRST TIME WE MET ONE ANOTHER'S

FAMILY WAS AMAZING BECAUSE

....

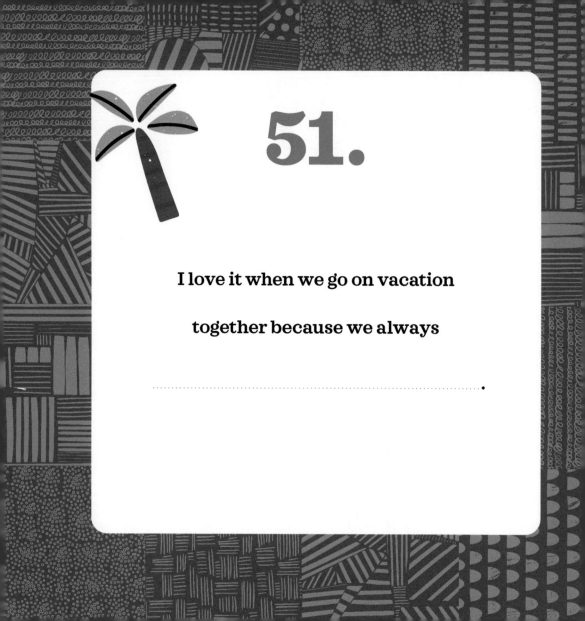

51.

I love it when we go on vacation

together because we always

....

52.

I laugh when I remember the time

we tried (and failed) to

....

53.

I LOVE TELLING PEOPLE ABOUT OUR

MOST UNFORGETTABLE ADVENTURE

WHEN WE

....

54.

I love that we can laugh together

about silly things like

....

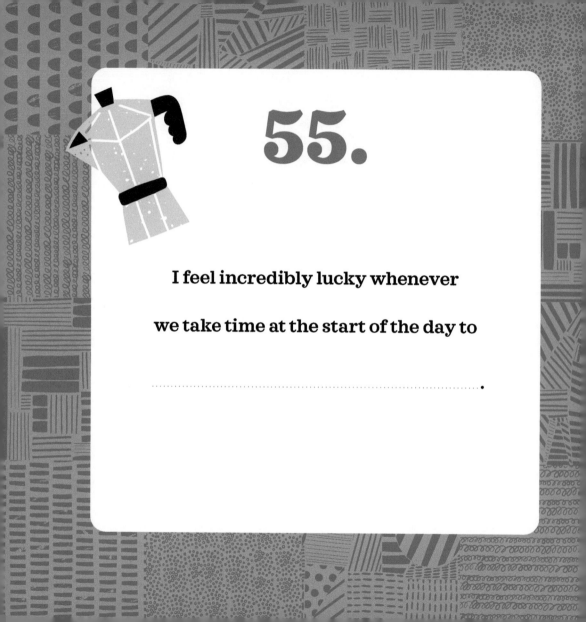

55.

I feel incredibly lucky whenever

we take time at the start of the day to

....

56.

Our top three funniest moments are

1. ....

2. ....

3. ....

57.

I look forward to our road trips because

. . . .

"extra love"

58.

My favorite photo of us is from the time we

....

because

....

59.

When one of us gets sick,

I love how we take care of each other by

. . . .

60.

I LOVE REMEMBERING THE FIRST TIME

WE EXCHANGED GIFTS, WHEN WE GAVE

EACH OTHER

....

61.

Something I truly treasure is the way

we appreciate each other's differences, like

....

62.

I appreciate how we keep our

schedules in sync by

....

63.

I love how our shared values about

....

connect us even more deeply.

64.

Our top three favorite, most relatable TV or movie couples are

1. ....

2. ....

3. ....

65.

I love when our favorite song comes on and we

....

I wouldn't want it any other way.

66.

I love that we make time for each

other when we're apart by

....

67.

I love that we give each other space to

....

68.

Our top three favorite snacks are

1. ....

2. ....

3. ....

69.

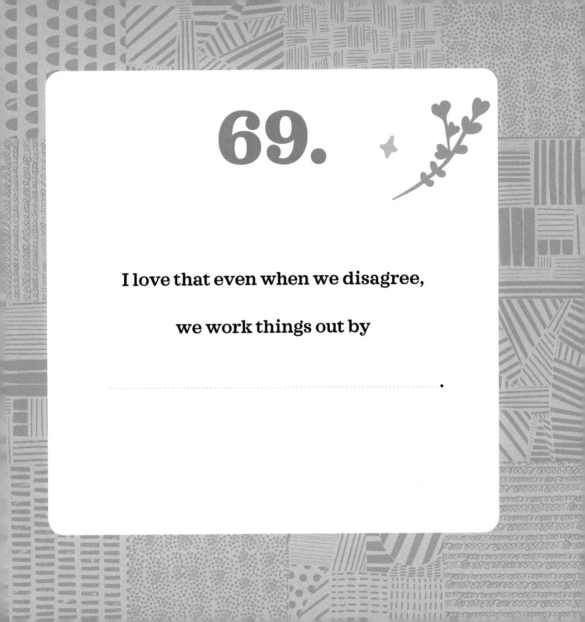

I love that even when we disagree,

we work things out by

....

70.

When times are stressful, I appreciate

how we support each other by

....

71.

I love how we each work on

our personal growth by

·

72.

♥ ♥ ♥ ♥

WHEN IT WAS TIME FOR OUR FIRST BIG

PURCHASE AS A COUPLE, I APPRECIATE

HOW WE

....

"extra love"

73.

I love that we prioritize each other

by never compromising on

. . . .

74.

I love how peaceful it feels when we

....

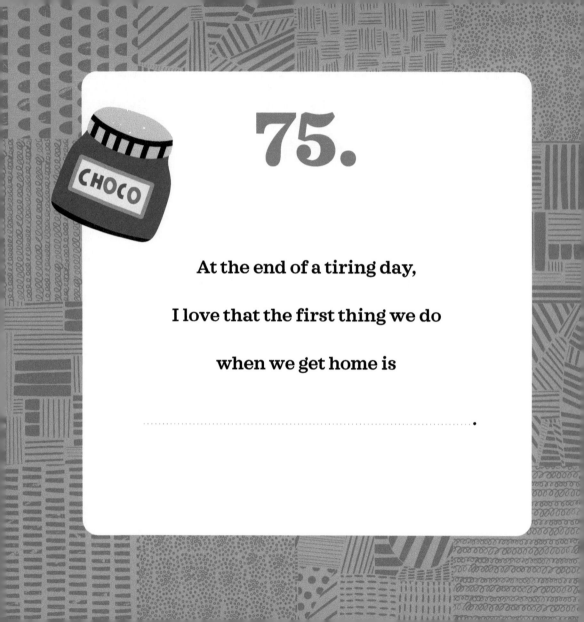

75.

At the end of a tiring day,

I love that the first thing we do

when we get home is

....

76.

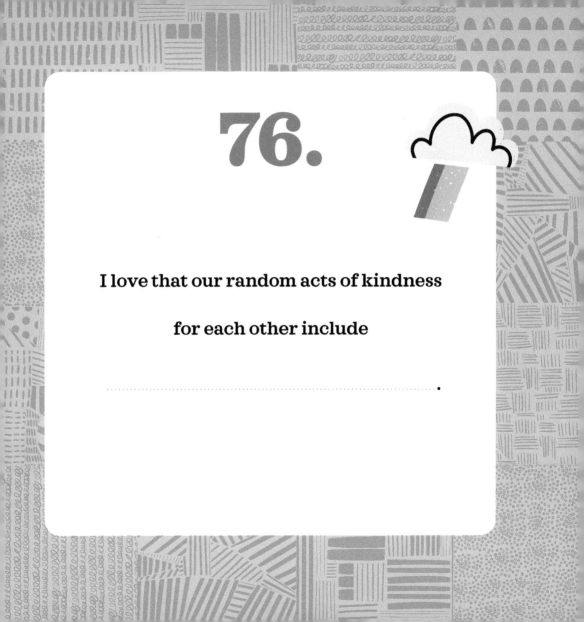

I love that our random acts of kindness

for each other include

....

77.

I love that your superpower is

....

YAY

78.

When we tell people the story of how

we met, we always make sure to include

....

79.

It was funny when we realized

that we both dislike

....

80.

The three most important things
our dream home will have are

1. ....

2. ....

3. ....

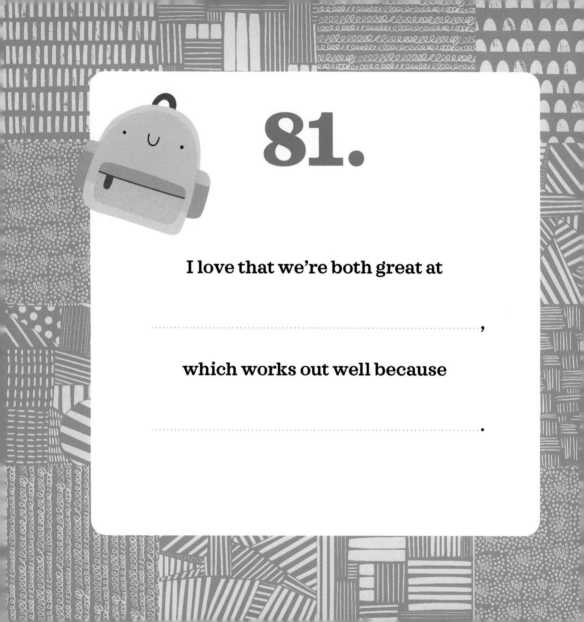

81.

I love that we're both great at

.... ,

which works out well because

....

82.

We both are terrible at

.... ,

so we always make sure to

....

83.

I love that we help each other

stay on track with our goals by

....

84.

I love when we show each other love

in unexpected ways, like the time

....

85.

I love that we soothe each other

during stressful times by

....

BRUSH.

86.

When we decide to stay in

for the night, I love when we

....

87.

Our personalities complement

each other brilliantly because

....

88.

I CHERISH THE MOMENT WE DECIDED

TO COMMIT TO EACH OTHER WHEN

89.

WHENEVER TIMES FEEL HARD,

I REMEMBER THE TOUGHEST MOMENT

THAT WE FACED TOGETHER WHEN WE

....

90.

It's so cute the way we

....

whenever

....

91.

I love that we respect one another's

opinions and how we ask each other's

advice about things like

....

92.

It means a lot to me that

we have healthy boundaries in our

relationship when it comes to

....

93.

I love the way we show each other affection by

....

94.

I WILL ALWAYS REMEMBER THE

MOMENT WE REUNITED AFTER BEING

APART DURING

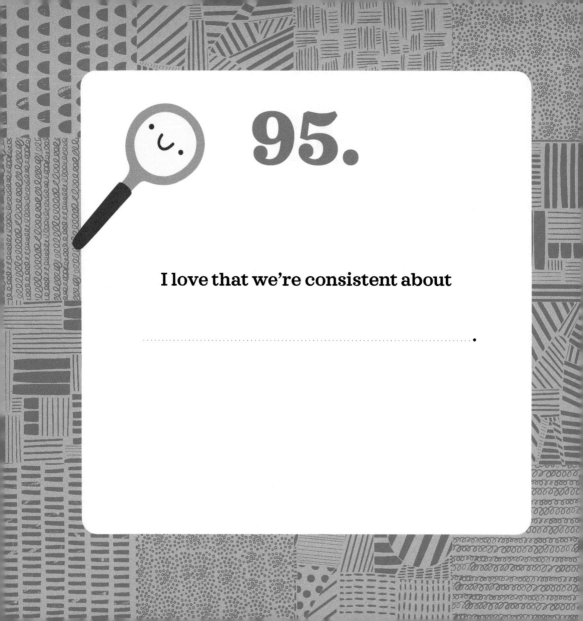

95.

I love that we're consistent about

....

96.

I love that we've decided to do good

in this world together by

.

97.

Our top three places to live one day are

1. ....

2. ....

3. ....

98.

I love that spending time together

never gets old with us, especially when we

....

99.

When we got together, I was relieved

when I realized that we both were great at

....

100.

I WILL ALWAYS REMEMBER THE TIME

WE HAD EACH OTHER'S BACKS WHEN

....

"extra love"